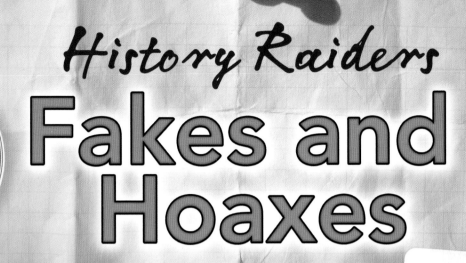

History Raiders
Fakes and Hoaxes

Sarah Eason

CRABTREE
PUBLISHING COMPANY
WWW.CRABTREEBOOKS.COM

Author: Sarah Eason
Editors: Jennifer Sanderson and Janine Deschenes
Proofreader and indexer: Tracey Kelly
Proofreader: Crystal Sikkens
Editorial director: Kathy Middleton
Design: Jessica Moon
Cover design: Katherine Berti
Photo research: Rachel Blount
Prepress and print coordination: Katherine Berti
Consultant: Rupert Matthews

Written, developed, and produced by Calcium

Library and Archives Canada Cataloguing in Publication

Title: Fakes and hoaxes / Sarah Eason.
Names: Eason, Sarah, author.
Description: Series statement: History raiders |
    Includes bibliographical references and index.
Identifiers: Canadiana (print) 20210192593 |
    Canadiana (ebook) 20210192607 |
    ISBN 9781427151049 (hardcover) |
    ISBN 9781427151100 (softcover) |
    ISBN 9781427151162 (HTML) |
    ISBN 9781427151223 (EPUB)
Subjects: LCSH: Hoaxes–Juvenile literature. |
    LCSH: Fraud in science–Juvenile literature. |
    LCSH: Curiosities and wonders–Juvenile literature.
Classification: LCC Q175.37 .E27 2022 | DDC j001.94–dc23

Library of Congress Cataloging-in-Publication Data

Available at the Library of Congress

Crabtree Publishing Company

www.crabtreebooks.com   1-800-387-7650

Copyright © **2022 CRABTREE PUBLISHING COMPANY**.
All rights reserved. No part of this publication may
be reproduced, stored in a retrieval system, or be
transmitted in any form or by any means, electronic,
mechanical, photocopying, recording, or otherwise,
without the prior written permission of Crabtree
Publishing Company. In Canada: We acknowledge the
financial support of the Government of Canada through
the Canada Book Fund for our publishing activities.

Published in Canada
Crabtree Publishing
616 Welland Ave.
St. Catharines, Ontario
L2M 5V6

Published in the United States
Crabtree Publishing
347 Fifth Ave
Suite 1402-145
New York, NY 10016

Printed in the U.S.A./062021/CG20210401

CONTENTS

TRICKY PAST

Many people love fascinating stories and intriguing mysteries. Perhaps that is why they are so eager to believe the fakes and hoaxes that others create. A fake is something that looks real, but it is not. It might be a story or an object. Hoaxes are tricks that deceive people into believing something that is not true.

Historical Pranks

Throughout history, people have created fakes and hoaxes. One example of a great historical fake is Drake's Plate. This is a brass marker that was found in 1936 in Northern California. At the time, people believed that it had belonged to the English explorer, Sir Francis Drake. They thought he had left it behind when he reached California in 1576. However, in 1977, scientific **analysis** proved that the plate was fake. It was then revealed that members of a historical group named the Clampers had created it as a practical joke.

Sir Francis Drake, shown right, never owned the brass marker! Yet, for years, people believed the fake had belonged to him.

Explore History

In this book, we will journey across the world to discover some of history's most impressive fakes and hoaxes. As we do so, we will examine questions raised by these amazing tricks. We will also gather **evidence** to explain why people were so easily fooled by them.

People love believing that creatures such as Bigfoot exist. Perhaps that is why they fall for hoaxes that encourage them to believe in the furry beast.

History Raider!

Hey! I'm Madison Maverick. I'm an explorer. I also like to think of myself as a history raider—a person who stops at nothing to find answers about the past. Come with me on my journeys to solve past mysteries and answer questions about history. Read my field notes on the History Raider pages and boxes. Then, jot down evidence to help solve each mystery.

MONSTROUS TRICKS

People have always been fascinated by stories of sea monsters. This may be because they know so little about the creatures that could lurk in Earth's oceans. Scientists estimate that as much as 91 percent of Earth's sea creatures are yet to be discovered. With so much to learn, it is no wonder that people have been convinced by tales of sea creatures—and fooled by watery tricks.

A Mermaid at the Museum

One such hoax was the case of the Fiji Mermaid. The mermaid was bought by P. T. Barnum from a U.S. sea captain named Samuel Edes. Barnum was the founder of Barnum's Circus and Barnum's American Museum. Even though experts said that the mermaid was not real, in 1842, Barnum put the mermaid on display in his museum. The mermaid was dubbed the Fiji Mermaid because she was supposedly caught near the Fiji Islands in the South Pacific Ocean. The mermaid was revealed to be a hoax. She was actually the skeleton of a monkey's head sewn onto the skeleton of a fish!

This is a model of Barnum's Fiji Mermaid, now on display in the Peabody Museum at Harvard University in Massachusetts.

The Monster of Loch Ness

For hundreds of years, people have been thrilled by the story of a huge, dinosaur-like monster named Nessie. Nessie is said to swim in **Loch** Ness in Scotland. Most scientists agree that there is no creature in the loch. However, many people still believe that a monster exists. They point to photographs as evidence (see pages 8 and 9).

People can sometimes see things they want to believe are true. For example, hundreds of years ago, sailors saw marine animals called manatees. They were convinced that the animals were mermaids! This was partly because they have long, flat tails, which make them look like mermaids.

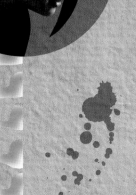

History Raider!

As I read more about the Loch Ness monster, I discovered one photograph that had convinced many people that Nessie was real. What was it about this picture that made people believe in the monster? And why had so many people been convinced by it? I had to find out.

History Raider!
Watery Monster

It was a cold, windy day at Loch Ness in the Scottish Highlands. I looked down at the photo I'd discovered, then across the water. The surface was calm. There was no sign of Nessie. I decided to head to the local library to see if there was more to the photograph than met the eye.

Nessie Lives!

As I searched online, I found that a number of sightings of Nessie were reported in the early 1930s. People everywhere became excited. They believed that maybe this Loch Ness monster was real. Then, in 1934, a photograph taken by a surgeon named Robert Wilson emerged. The photo showed a dinosaur-like creature in the loch. It was soon **published** in the British newspaper, *The Daily Mail*. Because a surgeon had taken the photo, people believed it was more credible.

Model Monster

In the years that followed, monster hunters flocked to the loch to try and find Nessie for themselves. They were convinced by Wilson's photo. However, in 1994, the photograph was proven to be a fake. The photo had been taken by a **big-game hunter** named Marmaduke Wetherell and his friend Christian Spurling. Wetherell and Spurling created a model of the monster out of a toy submarine and putty. They then gave the photo to their friend Robert Wilson to pass on to *The Daily Mail*.

Like this photo, Wilson's picture showed a long-necked creature that looked very much like a plesiosaur—a marine reptile that lived during the time of the dinosaurs.

Tricked or Trickster?

Why had Wetherell and Spurling done this? It seems that in the early 1930s, *The Daily Mail* had sent Wetherell to Scotland to track down the monster. As he searched along the shore of the lake, Wetherell discovered the tracks of a giant creature. However, it was later revealed that all he had discovered were fake prints. They were created by pranksters! The newspaper mocked Wetherell for his mistake and made him look foolish. Wetherell was determined to get back at them and prove that he was not the fool they believed him to be. He succeeded! He took a photograph that made people at the newspaper believe in the monster—and also the entire country!

Finding Answers

Wow—that was an amazing trip! Did you find evidence from my field notes that could help solve the puzzle of the loch? Turn to pages 28-29 to learn if your findings match mine!

9

A GIANT JOKE?

Throughout history, myths and fairy tales have featured giants and other huge creatures that once roamed Earth. These ideas have thrilled people and captured their imaginations. It is hardly surprising that in the past, when people have stumbled across giant bones, they have wondered if they might have belonged to giant, humanlike beings.

Bones and Books

There are many historical accounts of people finding huge bones in North America. Many believed that they had found the **remains** of giants. In 1705, a man named Cotton Mather from Massachusetts found **fossils** near Albany, New York. He believed the fossils were those of a giant. He thought the giant had died in the great flood written about in the **Bible**. Then, in 1835, a man named Josiah Priest published a book called *American Antiquities and Discoveries in the West*. In it, he claimed that bones found in Indiana were those of a long-gone group of giants. His book was a bestseller!

Could giants have roamed Earth thousands of years ago?

Using fossils and bones, modern scientists can identify many **species**, including dinosaurs and other **prehistoric** creatures.

Believing in Giants

Today, there are tools such as **DNA** analysis to help scientists identify bones and other remains. However, before such technology became available, it must have been easy to think that giants existed. It seemed even easier to trick people into believing it!

A Giant in Cardiff

In Cardiff, New York, in 1869, a big story broke. It told of two laborers who had been digging a well on a farm. While they were digging, they unearthed something spectacular…a giant! The 10-foot (3-m) figure had become **petrified** in the earth. News spread. Soon, **archaeologists** and onlookers gathered to find out about this mysterious creature.

History Raider!

When I researched the Cardiff Giant, I was intrigued. Why had so many people been convinced that the uncovered figure was a giant? How had their beliefs made them so sure it was real? It was time to investigate!

History Raider!
The Cardiff Giant

I headed straight to New York to the area where the Cardiff Giant had been found. I asked locals how I could learn more about this mysterious find. They recommended checking out a New York evening newspaper called *The Syracuse Journal.* It had reported on the discovery at the time.

Giant Wonder

I scanned the pages of the newspaper and read how people had rushed to see the body. Fossils had already been found in the area, so people believed that the body had become petrified in a nearby swamp. The owner of the farm, William Newell, set up a tent on the farm. He displayed the body for 25 cents per visitor.

People flocked to see the petrified giant at the Farmer's Museum in Cooperstown, New York.

TALLER THAN GOLIATH WHOM DAVID

10 FEET 4 1/2 INCHES TALL — WEIGHT 2990 L

SIX MILLION PEOPLE HAVE PAID TO SEE HIM. DAVID HARUM WAS *HIS* GOD FATHER

P.T. BARNUM OFFERED $150000 FOR THE GIANT

THE MOST VALUABLE SINGLE EXHIBIT IN THE WORLD TODAY

THE GREAT
CARDIFF GIANT
PHENOMENON
OF THE CENTURY!

A Giant Fake

My research soon led me to comments by archaeologists and other experts. Some said that the giant was a remarkable find, but others said it was fake. One pointed out that the body was made of gypsum, a type of white powder, and not bone. Another said that there were recent tool marks on the body, proving it could not be real. Yet another expert questioned why the laborers had been digging a well in that exact spot, since there was no water source there. However, none of their comments kept people from flocking to see the giant and believing it was the real thing.

The True Story

Eventually, I came across the truth. I learned that Newell's cousin, George Hull, had wanted to prove how easy it was to fool the public, especially followers of Christianity. He claimed they would believe that the giant was real because a version of the Bible said that giantlike people had once lived on Earth. Hull also saw the fake giant as a way to make some money. He ordered a huge statue to be made and had it buried on the farm. A year later, he told the two laborers to dig in that very spot to unearth the body!

Finding Answers

Wow! That was a believable hoax! I think I have the answers to my questions now. What do your notes show? Turn to pages 28–29 to learn if your findings match mine!

FAIRY FUN

Fairies are said to be magical beings. Stories about them date back thousands of years. Many people still find fairy stories mystical and enchanting**. Some people believe fairies are real—and claim to have seen them.**

Fairies Forever

Over the centuries, many people claim to have seen fairies or have said that they believed in them. There are writings from **medieval** times about fairies that appeared as dwarf creatures in green clothes or as tiny, winged women. In the 1300s, an English lawyer and writer named Gervase of Tilbury claimed that fairies lived in enchanted places. The stories about fairies continued through the centuries that followed.

Fairies are often described as being dainty with fluttering wings, dancing in rings, and being surrounded by a glowing light.

Investigating Fairies

Many stories about fairies were told in the 1920s, after World War I (1914-1918). During this time, fairy stories became particularly popular because people wanted to escape the horrors of the war. People loved to read these tales of fantasy and mystery. Fairies were so intriguing that in England, United Kingdom (U.K.), a group was set up to investigate them. It was called the Fairy Investigation Society. One of its most famous members was the entrepreneur Walt Disney. Sir Arthur Conan Doyle, creator of the character Sherlock Holmes, was another member of the Fairy Investigation Society. He published photographs that seemed to show fairies dancing. This made people even more excited. The photographs became known as the Cottingley Fairy photographs.

Stories of fairies still fill children's bookshelves around the world.

History Raider!

I am amazed by the Cottingley Fairy photographs. They look so realistic! How were they created, and why did people believe in them so strongly? I had to find out more about this fascinating fairy tale.

History Raider!
Fooled by Fairies

My research took me to the town of Cottingley near Bradford, England. In 1917, so the story goes, two little girls were playing by a stream in their large backyard. There, they took photos of fairies. The photos caused a sensation across the country.

Fairy Photos

The girls were cousins Elsie Wright, who was 16 years old, and Frances Griffiths, age 9. After taking the photographs, the two girls showed them to their parents. Elsie's father thought they were fake, but her mother believed they were real. She showed them to friends and other people. Eventually, the photos ended up in the hands of Sir Arthur Conan Doyle. Conan Doyle believed in the **supernatural** and thought the photos were real.

Conan Doyle believed the photos were proof that other fantasy worlds existed. Fans of his were eager to agree.

Famous Fairies

I found a copy of *The Strand* magazine containing an article written by Conan Doyle on fairies. It was illustrated with the photos. The public loved the work of Conan Doyle and admired his ideas. His article made the Cottingley Fairies famous. It made the idea of them being real even more believable.

Keeping to the Story

After the photographs were made public, the cousins insisted the photos were real. But as I dug deeper, I learned about a man named Joe Cooper. He was a firm believer in the Cottingley Fairies. In the 1970s, he began writing to Elsie to find out more about her magical photographs. He finally met with Elsie. At their meeting, he learned the truth behind the photos.

Fake Fairies!

Elsie shattered Cooper's long-held belief that the photos were real. She told him they were fake. She explained that the fairies were simply pictures cut out of magazines with drawn wings pasted on. Elsie said the images had been just a childish trick—but it was one that had fooled the world for years.

Finding Answers

The fairy photographs were so good, they almost had me fooled, too! All the evidence I gathered from my investigation has helped answer my questions. What did you record? Turn to pages 28–29 to find out if your findings match mine!

A MISSING LINK?

It is believed that while humans and apes evolved **alongside each other, both share a common ancestor. The species is known as the Last Common Ancestor (LCA), or the missing link. Over time, many people have claimed they have found it.**

Super Prank

In 1958, a trail of supersized footprints found in Northern California was reported in a local newspaper. The idea of the creature that made the tracks quickly created a lot of excitement. Soon, people, including scientists, began to wonder if the creature could be real. They thought it was possibly the missing link. However, in 2002, it was claimed that the giant footprints were made by a man named Ray Wallace. When Wallace died, his children said their father had created the prints long ago by making giant wooden feet. He then stamped them into the ground.

Humans are closely related to apes. However, no one has found proof of a creature that is half human and half ape.

Bigfoot, Big Mystery

Since the 1950s, there have been claimed sightings of a huge, hairy beast hiding in forests across North America. The mysterious monster has become known as Bigfoot. Many believe that Bigfoot is the missing link. Photos, videos, footprints, and even skin and hair that are said to belong to Bigfoot have been found.

The Piltdown Puzzle

Between 1911 and 1912, jaw and skull bones were discovered in the village of Piltdown, in Sussex, England. The man who found them claimed they were part of a skull belonging to an ancient human. He named him Piltdown Man. The man also claimed he had found the missing link between apes and humans.

A Bigfoot road sign in Pikes Peak, Colorado, keeps the myth alive!

BIG FOOT XING

DUE TO SIGHTINGS IN THE AREA OF A CREATURE RESEMBLING "BIG FOOT" THIS SIGN HAS BEEN POSTED FOR YOUR SAFETY

History Raider!

I was fascinated by the idea of a missing link in human evolution, so I dug deeper to learn more about the Piltdown Man. What was it about this discovery that had convinced people they had found the missing link? And why was finding the missing link so important in England at this time? Time to find out.

19

History Raider!
The Piltdown Man

My research took me to the Natural History Museum in London, England. This is where the **amateur** archaeologist, Charles Dawson, sent the Piltdown bones when he found them. He claimed he had dug them up in old gravel pits near the village of Piltdown in Sussex. The pits dated from the **Pleistocene** period.

Fit Together

I learned that the museum had pieced together the bones. Experts there had noted that the skull resembled a human skull. The teeth could have been human or ape. The fossils were the same reddish-brown color as the gravel in the pits. This seemed to prove that the bones also dated from the Pleistocene period. Experts claimed this was all evidence of a human that had lived 500,000 years ago.

Not so Old!

Then, in the 1950s, scientists used new chemical tests to check the age of the bones. The tests revealed that the bones were no more than 720 years old. This proved they could not be the missing link. Further tests revealed that some of the bones belonged to a human, but others belonged to an ape, probably an orangutan. More tests showed that there were scratches on the teeth. They had been filed down to look like human teeth. This proved once and for all that Piltdown Man was a fake.

Hi-Tech Tests

I wondered what scientists today think about the Piltdown Man. I discovered tests performed in 2009 by an **anthropologist** named Isabelle De Groote. She and her team took a DNA **sample** from the teeth of Piltdown Man. They used **computer tomography (CT)** scanning to compare it with the DNA of apes. The tests confirmed that the teeth really did come from an orangutan. The CT scans also revealed that putty and gravel had been placed in some of the bones and teeth. De Groote's team believed this was done to make the bones weigh more. Ancient fossilized bones are heavier than more recent bones, so this made the bones seem more realistic.

In the 1900s, scientists in England desperately wanted to believe in the Piltdown Man to keep up with fossil discoveries being made in other countries, such as Germany.

Finding Answers

So, no missing link—yet! I have made a note of all the evidence that answers my questions about Piltdown Man. What do your notes show? Turn to pages 28–29 to learn if your findings match mine!

THE RUSSIAN PRINCESS

During World War I, more than 3,000,000 Russian soldiers died. And after the war, there was further hardship in Russia. Despite this, the rich and powerful of Russia lived in luxury. The Russian people blamed their leader, Czar Nicholas II, for their troubles. They believed he was ignoring their desperate need for work and food.

Death of the Czar

In 1918, the Russian people turned against the Czar in the Russian Revolution. They were led by a **communist** group called the Bolsheviks. The Czar and his family were arrested by the Bolsheviks. They were held prisoner in a basement. There, they were executed, or killed.

Burned and Buried

News soon spread that the royal family had been killed and their bodies burned and buried. However, no evidence of this was found. Rumors spread that some of the family had escaped. There were even stories that the girls had survived. People whispered that the bullets fired at them had bounced off jewelry hidden in their clothes.

Bolsheviks aim their guns to try and kill the Czar and those who were loyal to him.

I Am Anastasia!

After the Czar and his family were murdered, all of their great wealth was locked away in a bank vault. The riches belonged to any surviving relatives of the Czar. Unsurprisingly, in the years that followed, a number of women came forward, all claiming to be the Czar's youngest daughter, Princess Anastasia. One of them in particular convinced many people that she was the escaped princess. Her name was Anastasia Tschaikovsky.

The Czar and his wife had five children. Anastasia (on the right) was the youngest.

History Raider!

The story of Anastasia Tschaikovsky is fascinating. I wondered how she convinced people that she was the Czar's youngest daughter. What was it about her story that was so convincing? I knew I had to find out.

History Raider!
Anastasia's Story

As I looked into the story, I learned that it began in a German **mental asylum** in 1922. There, a young woman named Anastasia Tschaikovsky declared that she was Russia's Princess Anastasia.

Anna in America

I discovered that in 1928, Anastasia Tschaikovsky left Germany for New York City. She changed her name to Anna Anderson. In America, she was welcomed by Russians who believed her story—including the son of the Czar's family doctor, who was executed with them. Her supporters claimed that she knew details about life in Russia and had a strong resemblance to the princess.

The Real Anna

However, not everyone had believed Anna's story, including Princess Anastasia's uncle, the Grand Duke of Hesse. He hired a detective to look into Anna's claim. The detective said that Anna was really a woman named Franziska Schanzkowska, a factory worker from Poland. However, Anna still claimed she was Anastasia. What was the truth?

I headed to the library to find out more. Reports showed that Anna Anderson was still claiming to be Anastasia when she died in 1984. However, years later, scientists compared DNA from her body with that of Karl Maucher, a great nephew of Franziska Schanzkowska. The DNA proved that Anna's story was a lie.

Another Mystery Solved

Next, I learned that between the late 1990s and 2007, all of the bodies of the Czar and his family were finally found. They were identified through DNA testing, proving once more that there were no surviving members of the Russian royal family.

Anna Anderson's age, looks, and education all seemed to fit with that of the real princess, shown here. She even had scars on her body that she claimed the Bolshevik soldiers had made with their bullets.

Finding Answers

That was a real mystery story! I can now understand why so many people believed Anna was Anastasia. What did you note down? Turn to pages 28–29 to learn if your findings match mine!

ONGOING MYSTERIES

Advances in technology will help scientists and other experts identify hoaxes and fakes from history more accurately. Using new techniques, they can determine the age and composition **of bones and** artifacts**. This will make them better able to solve mysteries of the future.**

Old Bones

Carbon dating is a way of finding out how old living things are. Carbon is a chemical element found in all living things. One type of carbon, called carbon-14, starts to decay, or rot, when a living thing dies. Experts measure how much carbon is left in the object. This tells them how old the object is.

Chemical Tests

Isotopes are tiny **atoms** found in all living things. They contain all kinds of information about living things, such as what they ate and what the **climate** was like when they lived. Experts give a very small piece of bone a series of chemical tests. The results of the tests can tell if the discovery, such as the Piltdown Man, is a recent hoax or a real find from thousands of years ago.

Advances in technology mean that today, it is very hard to fake stories like the Piltdown Man.

It's in the DNA

Experts can use DNA testing to find out the truth about living things. This is what they did with Anna Anderson, who claimed to be Princess Anastasia. Except for identical twins, who share DNA, each person's DNA is unique and not found in any other living thing. By testing DNA from one set of bones and comparing it with another set, experts can tell if the DNA belongs to the same person or if the person is related to others.

Seeing the Invisible

For many years, microscopes have been used to examine the surface of objects. The tools enable experts to see things that are invisible to the **naked eye**. Today's powerful microscopes have been developed to allow experts to see inside an object as well, without having to cut or damage it to investigate.

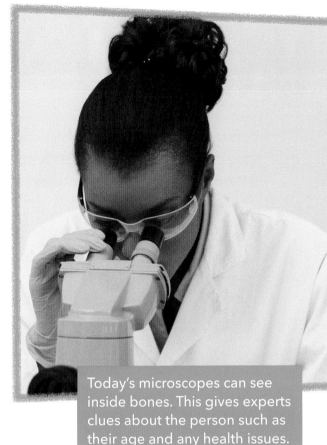

Today's microscopes can see inside bones. This gives experts clues about the person such as their age and any health issues.

History Raider!

For adventurers like us, the world is full of mysteries to explore. The history of fakes and hoaxes has been so much fun to discover, and I can't wait to uncover the truth about future tricks that are sure to come!

27

MYSTERY SOLVED?

Some of those fakes and hoaxes were quite believable, weren't they? After gathering the evidence, here are some conclusions I made after each journey. How do yours match up?

Pages 8-9: Watery Monster

It's surprising that a photograph could fool so many people into believing in the Loch Ness monster. People believed that Robert Wilson's photograph was genuine. This is because Wilson was a surgeon, so he seemed more credible. The photo was published in a national newspaper.

Pages 12-13: The Cardiff Giant

There was a lot of "evidence" that seemed to prove the Cardiff giant was real. Fossils had been found in the area, so people believed that the body had become petrified in the nearby swamp. Many religious men said the body was real. They even quoted Bible passages to prove this. However, the Cardiff giant was proven to be fake.

Pages 16-17: Fooled by Fairies

The truth about the fairy pictures was amazing! The fairy photos were actually pictures cut out of magazines with drawn wings pasted on. People loved the work of Conan Doyle and admired his ideas. His article about the Cottingley Fairies made them famous and even more believable.

Pages 20-21: The Piltdown Man

There were several reasons why people believed that the Piltdown Man was the missing link. The fossils were the same color as the gravel in the pits. The skull resembled a human skull. The teeth could be human or ape. Scientists in England wanted to believe in the Piltdown Man to keep up with fossil discoveries in other countries.

Pages 24-25: Anastasia's Story

Anna's story was so convincing, and her supporters helped make her story believable! She knew so much about the real Anastasia that many people believed her. Her age, looks, and education all seemed to fit with that of the real Anastasia. She also had scars on her body. She claimed these were made by the Bolshevik soldiers.

GLOSSARY

amateur Someone who does something as a hobby rather than as a paid job

analysis Detailed examination

anthropologist Someone who studies societies and their cultures

archaeologists People who study history through artifacts and remains

artifacts Objects that were made by people in the past

atoms The smallest units of matter

Bible The holy book used by Christians

big-game hunter Someone who hunts large animals, such as lions

climate The weather conditions in an area over a long period of time

communist Describes a person or country where all property is owned by the community, and each person contributes and receives according to their ability and needs

composition What something is made from

computer tomography (CT) A type of X-ray that sends pictures from inside an object to a computer screen

DNA The substance in cells that carries unique information about living things

enchanting Charming

evidence A sign that shows that something exists or is true

evolved To have changed slowly over many thousands of years

fossils The remains of living things that have been preserved in rock

loch A lake or a bay mostly surrounded by land

medieval Describes the time between 500 and 1500 C.E.

mental asylum A psychiatric hospital of the past where people with mental illnesses were treated

naked eye Describes looking at something without using anything to make the object bigger

petrified Changed into a stone over a long period of time

Pleistocene A period in time millions of years ago

prehistoric Before written records

published On sale to the public, usually in the form of a book

remains Pieces or parts of something that are left when most of it has been used up or destroyed

sample A small amount of something, usually used in testing

species A group of closely related living things

supernatural Describes something caused by forces that cannot be explained by science

LEARNING MORE

BOOKS

Finding Bigfoot: Everything You Need To Know. Animal Planet, 2013.

Dyer, Janice. *Haunted Woods and Caves* (Haunted or Hoax?). Crabtree Publishing Company, 2018.

Jazynka, Kitson. *History's Mysteries: Freaky Phenomena: Curious Clues, Cold Cases, and Puzzles from the Past.* National Geographic Kids, 2018.

Pascoe, Elaine. *Fooled You!: Fakes and Hoaxes Through the Years.* Square Fish, 2016.

WEBSITES

Learn about the life of Princess Anastasia, her death, and the woman who claimed to be the missing princess at:
https://kids.kiddle.co/Grand_Duchess_Anastasia_Nikolaevna_of_Russia

Find out more about Bigfoot at:
https://kids.kiddle.co/Bigfoot

Discover more about the Loch Ness monster, and take a look at the place where Nessie is said to have been seen at:
https://kids.kiddle.co/Loch_Ness

Join the experts as they explain how Piltdown Man was revealed to be a hoax at:
www.nhm.ac.uk/discover/news/2016/august/piltdown-man-charles-dawson-likely-fraudster

INDEX

About the Author

Sarah Eason has written many books for children. Through researching this book, she has discovered that some of the world's most thrilling mysteries can be explained through science, and that people will go to almost any length to fool others into believing in magic and wonder!